OUT IN FRONT

MALALA YOUSAFZAI
AND THE GIRLS
OF PAKISTAN

MALALA
YOUSAFZAI
ARRIVES
AT A PRESS
CONFERENCE
AT HARVARD
UNIVERSITY IN
SEPTEMBER 2013.

OUT IN FRONT

MALALA YOUSAFZAI
AND THE GIRLS
OF PAKISTAN

DAVID ARETHA

MORGAN REYNOLDS
PUBLISHING

GREENSBORO, NORTH CAROLINA

To join the discussion about this title, please check out the Morgan Reynolds Readers Club on Facebook, or Like our company page to stay up to date on the latest Morgan Reynolds news!

PAKISTANI SCHOOLGIRLS
PRAY FOR THE RECOVERY OF
MALALA YOUSAFZAI, SHOT
BY A TALIBAN ASSASSIN.

Library of Congress Cataloging-in-Publication Data

Aretha, David.
 Malala Yousafzai and the girls of Pakistan / by David Aretha.
   pages cm. -- (Out in front)
 Includes bibliographical references and index.
  ISBN 978-1-59935-454-5 -- ISBN 978-1-59935-455-2 (e-book)
 1. Yousafzai, Malala, 1997---Juvenile literature. 2. Girls--Education--Pakistan-
-Juvenile literature. 3. Sex discrimination in education--Pakistan--Juvenile
literature. 4. Women social reformers--Pakistan--Biography--Juvenile literature.
5. Social reformers--Pakistan--Biography--Juvenile literature. 6. Political
activists--Pakistan--Biography--Juvenile literature. 7. Girls--Violence against--
Pakistan--Juvenile literature. 8. Taliban--Juvenile literature. 9. Pakistan--Social
conditions--Juvenile literature. I. Title.
 LC2330.A74 2014
 371.822095491--dc23
                        2013044510

Printed in the United States of America
First Edition

Book cover and interior designed by:
Ed Morgan, navyblue design studio
Greensboro, NC

CONTENTS

CHAPTER ONE:
The Girl Who Couldn't Be Silenced

تندی بادِ مخالف سے نہ گھبرا اے عقاب
یہ تو چلتی ہے تجھے اونچا اڑانے کے لئے

ملالہ کیلئے پوری قوم دعا گو

سٹی ڈسٹرکٹ گورنمنٹ لاہور

PAKISTANIS
HOLD A
CANDLELIGHT
VIGIL FOR
MALALA IN
LAHORE,
PAKISTAN.

In October 2012, a Taliban gunman shoved a Colt .45 pistol through the window of a school bus and shot Malala Yousafzai in the head. Finally, the shooter believed, the outspoken Pakistani teen had been silenced. The girl had delivered a speech entitled "How dare the Taliban take away my basic right to education." Now, she was surely dead.

The gunman was wrong. Malala survived. And on July 12, 2013, her sixteenth birthday, the courageous heroine stood on a podium at the United Nations headquarters to trumpet her message to the world. "The terrorists thought that they would change our aims and stop our ambitions," she said, "but nothing changed in my life except this: Weakness, fear, and hopelessness died. Strength, power, and courage was born."

In Malala's home of Swat Valley, Pakistan, the Taliban—an Islamic fundamentalist group that rules by force—had blown up more than a hundred girls schools. Now, in an event described as Malala Day, the spokesperson for the right to education addressed world dignitaries and the five hundred young people in attendance.

"The extremists are afraid of books and pens," Malala declared with conviction. "The power of education frightens them. They are afraid of women. The power of the voice of women frightens them. . . . That is why they are blasting schools every day—because they were and they are afraid of change, afraid of the equality that we will bring into our society."

Malala stated that in many parts of the world, particularly Pakistan and Afghanistan, wars and terrorism prevent children from going to their schools. Across the world, more than 50 million

MALALA
YOUSAFZAI
DELIVERS
A SPEECH
AT THE UN
HEADQUARTERS
IN NEW YORK.

children, mostly girls, are denied access to education. She discussed other issues facing the world's youth: "In India, innocent and poor children are victims of child labor. Many schools have been destroyed in Nigeria. People in Afghanistan have been affected by the hurdles of extremism for decades. Young girls have to do domestic child labor and are forced to get married at early age."

Addressing world leaders, Malala voiced the demands of the more than 1 million people who had signed her petition. "We call upon the world leaders that all the peace deals must protect women and children's rights," she declared. "We call upon all governments to ensure free compulsory education for every child all over the world. We call upon all governments to fight against terrorism and violence, to protect children from brutality and harm. We call upon the developed nations to support the expansion of educational opportunities for girls in the developing world."

Before leaving to a standing ovation, Malala concluded:

SO LET US WAGE A GLOBAL STRUGGLE AGAINST ILLITERACY, POVERTY, AND TERRORISM AND LET US PICK UP OUR BOOKS AND PENS. THEY ARE OUR MOST POWERFUL WEAPONS. ONE CHILD, ONE TEACHER, ONE PEN, AND ONE BOOK CAN CHANGE THE WORLD. EDUCATION IS THE ONLY SOLUTION. EDUCATION FIRST.

World leaders have been listening to the pleas of Malala, who in 2013 was nominated for the Nobel Peace Prize (had she won, she would have been the youngest-ever recipient) and won the prestigious Sakharov Prize for her contribution to human rights. In December 2012, the cash-strapped Pakistani government committed $10 million to the Malala Fund for Girls' Education. Gordon Brown, the UN special envoy for global education, set a goal to get every child in the world in school by 2015. "Malala says it is possible," Brown said, "and young people all over the world think it is possible."

Rarely in history has a child affected national and international policies like this teenager from Pakistan. Then again, rarely has there been a girl like Malala—highly educated and intelligent, charismatic and compassionate, humble and likable. She has also been called, by *CNN* and others, the bravest girl in the world.

CHAPTER TWO:
Trouble in Paradise

SWAT VALLEY, WHERE MALALA YOUSAFZAI WAS RAISED.

On July 12, 1997, a child was born in Mingora, Pakistan, to a woman named Toorpakai Yousafzai. Named after a courageous Afghan heroine, Malala Yousafzai entered the world kicking and screaming. Ziauddin, her father, beamed with pride. "He says he looked into my eyes after I was born and fell in love," Malala wrote. "He told people, 'I know there is something different about this child.'"

Ziauddin Yousafzai was a different kind of father. Though the education of women was not highly valued in much of the Muslim world, Ziauddin would one day run a network of schools, including those exclusively for girls. Malala, his first child, would be educated.

When Malala was born, Ziauddin ran just one small school, and the Yousafzai family lived across the street from it in a two-room shack. "We had no bathroom or kitchen," Malala wrote, "and my mother cooked on a wood fire on the ground and washed our clothes at a tap in the school."

Though Mingora was a bustling, crowded, and largely dirty city of 170,000, it rested in the beautiful Swat Valley. Snow-capped mountains, lush valleys, roaring waterfalls, sparkling lakes, and rivers full of trout earned Swat the nickname "Paradise of Pakistan." "Our valley is full of fruit trees on which grow the sweetest figs and pomegranates and peaches," Malala wrote.

From an early age, Malala loved her natural surroundings and enjoyed going to school. She spent her pocket money on books, including a biography of Benazir Bhutto (Pakistan's first female prime minister), and loaded her books in a Harry Potter backpack. By age eleven, she had read Stephen Hawkings's *A Brief History of Time*, and she dreamed of one day becoming a doctor or perhaps an inventor. "She was precocious, confident, assertive," said local politician Adnan Aurangzeb. "A young person with the drive to achieve something in life."

For a Pakistani girl, Malala was more fortunate than most. In Pakistan, the sixth-largest country in the world (193 million people), the per-capita annual income is less than $3,000 in U.S. dollars, which ranks 178th in the world, according to the Central Intelligence Agency (CIA). Internal and external conflicts have long plagued this Muslim country, resulting in political instability and often substandard public utilities. Pakistan's literacy rate is very low, just 69 percent for males and 40 percent for females, according to the CIA.

MINGORA, PAKISTAN

Education in the country is in a particularly dismal state. Approximately 7 million children are not in school, and according to a 2009 report, Pakistan has the largest out-of-school population in the world after Nigeria and India, accounting for 7 percent of global absentees. In rural and poverty stricken areas, education is largely not a priority: the children are needed to work and help provide for the family, or are simply too hungry to attend school.

Things are especially dire for girls. In some rural and tribal areas, education of girls is strictly prohibited on religious grounds. In other areas, though educating girls is not forbidden, it is not allowed for girls to attend school with boys; there are, however, far fewer schools for girls.

A GIRL ATTENDS SCHOOL IN QUTBAL, PAKISTAN.

Malala's home of Swat Valley, however, had a proud history of education. In the 1920s, when Swat was a semi-autonomous region, ruler Miangul Gulshahzada Sir Abdul Wadud laid the construction for a network of schools in the valley, including girls' schools. In the second half of the century, Swat produced an impressive number of professionals, including many female doctors and teachers.

Swat was a relatively peaceful place when Malala was born, but all that changed after September 11, 2001. Following the terrorist attacks in the United States on that day, the U.S. targeted the culprit—a militant Islamist organization called al-Qaeda. In Afghanistan, the Taliban harbored al-Qaeda operatives, and the U.S. military and its allies targeted them as well.

The U.S. military invasion of Afghanistan triggered a backlash—a swelling tide of anti-American, anti-Western sentiment among Muslims in Afghanistan and its neighbor just to the east, Pakistan. Working out of Swat Valley, Sufi Muhammad Khan, leader of a Taliban-aligned group, led 10,000 men into Afghanistan to fight the U.S. forces.

In Swat, the heavily armed Taliban gained a stronger and stronger hold—a situation that deeply troubled most of its residents as well as the Pakistani government. From 1996 to 2001, the Taliban had ruled most of Afghanistan, wreaking havoc across that country. The Taliban brought about order in Afghanistan through an ultra-strict interpretation of Islamic law. Television, the Internet, and music were banned. Opponents were beaten or executed. Access to food and water declined, and the Taliban prevented United Nations relief supplies from getting to Afghanistan's starving citizens. Moreover, the Taliban severely oppressed women's rights. Girls were not allowed to go to school, and women were barred from working outside the home, causing a crisis in education and health care. A woman who left home without the company of a male relative risked being beaten or shot. Thousands of young Afghan widows, barred from working, were forced to beg on the streets.

PAKISTANI
SOLDIERS STAND
GUARD IN MINGORA.

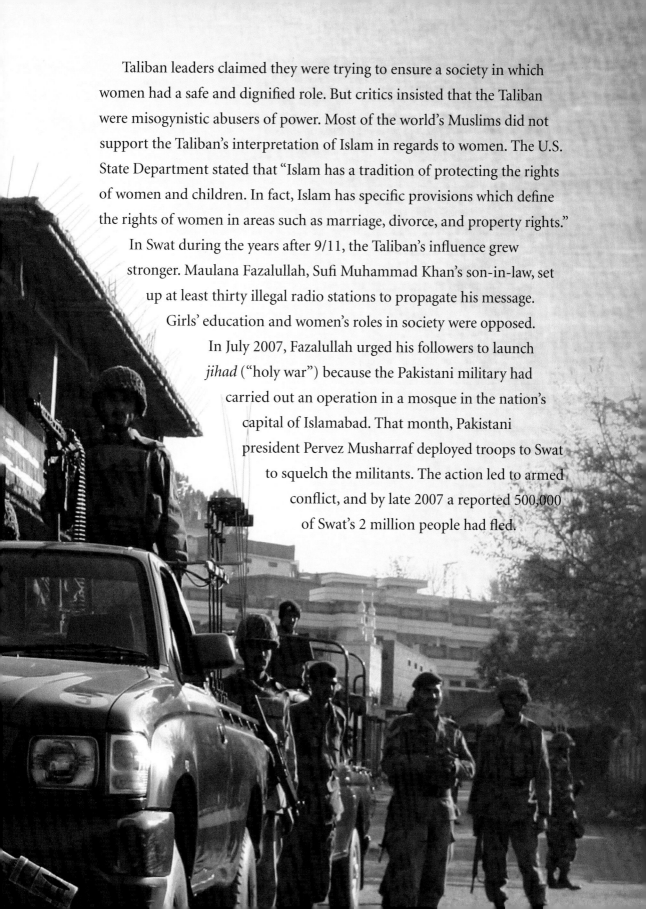

Taliban leaders claimed they were trying to ensure a society in which women had a safe and dignified role. But critics insisted that the Taliban were misogynistic abusers of power. Most of the world's Muslims did not support the Taliban's interpretation of Islam in regards to women. The U.S. State Department stated that "Islam has a tradition of protecting the rights of women and children. In fact, Islam has specific provisions which define the rights of women in areas such as marriage, divorce, and property rights."

In Swat during the years after 9/11, the Taliban's influence grew stronger. Maulana Fazalullah, Sufi Muhammad Khan's son-in-law, set up at least thirty illegal radio stations to propagate his message. Girls' education and women's roles in society were opposed.

In July 2007, Fazalullah urged his followers to launch *jihad* ("holy war") because the Pakistani military had carried out an operation in a mosque in the nation's capital of Islamabad. That month, Pakistani president Pervez Musharraf deployed troops to Swat to squelch the militants. The action led to armed conflict, and by late 2007 a reported 500,000 of Swat's 2 million people had fled.

The violence escalated in 2008. Military tanks rolled through the streets, and the Taliban killed women who refused to quit their jobs. By the end of the year, some 150 schools had been destroyed, and thousands of girls, out of fear, stopped going to school.

Malala was not one of them. In September 2008, the eleven-year-old girl and her father spoke on a radio show. "How dare the Taliban take away my basic right to education," Malala said.

The Taliban infringed on Malala's life in many ways. Because the remote areas of Swat were less safe than Mingora, some of Malala's cousins moved in with her family. The crowded home got on her nerves, and the children couldn't go outside and play cricket like they used to. "We played marbles in the yard over and over again," Malala wrote. "I fought nonstop with my brother Khushal, and he would go crying to our mother."

Malala spent hours in the bathroom trying different hairstyles, only to have her mother tell her to hurry up—their guests needed to use the bathroom, too. Like many young girls, Malala fretted about her looks. "I was really worried about my height," she once remarked. "I said, 'I'll never grow up, I'm never going to be taller.'"

Mostly, though, Malala worried about the Taliban.

Late that year, Aamer Ahmed Khan of the BBC Urdu Web site was looking for a blogger to write about conditions in Swat Valley. When a candidate backed out, Ziauddin recommended his young daughter. BBC editors agreed, and on January 3, 2009, Malala—under the pseudonym "Gul Makai" ("cornflower")—wrote her first entry. She handwrote the words in her native Urdu, and they were scanned and sent by e-mail to the BBC editors.

Malala wrote that of the twenty-seven students in her class, only eleven had attended school the previous day. In that first blog, she gave readers a sense of the tension in the city: "On my way from school to home I heard a man saying 'I will kill you.' I hastened my pace and after a while I looked back if the man was still coming behind me. But to my utter relief he was talking on his mobile and must have been threatening someone else over the phone."

Malala, who has two younger brothers, wrote about her home life, shopping, and school. She bemoaned how the family no longer could picnic in the valley on Sundays due to the military operations. She also noted that the Taliban had announced a ban on girls' education in Swat beginning January 15, which greatly displeased her.

A sense of hopelessness pervaded Malala's January 14 blog entry. "Since today was the last day of our school, we decided to play in the playground a bit longer," she wrote. "I am of the view that the school will one day reopen but while leaving I looked at the building as if I would not come here again."

BENAZIR BHUTTO

When Malala addressed world leaders at the headquarters of the United Nations, she wore a shawl once owned by her hero: Benazir Bhutto. Not just Pakistan's first female prime minister, but one of the Middle East's most complex and influential leaders, Benazir Bhutto was born in Pakistan in June of 1953. She was the daughter of Zulfikar Ali Bhutto, a prominent Pakistani politician.

As a child, Benazir attended the best schools, and at age sixteen left home to attend Harvard's Radcliffe College and then England's Oxford University. Meanwhile, her father was elected prime minister of Pakistan in 1971, and his beloved daughter Benazir accompanied him on many important political trips and meetings.

After completing her studies in politics and economics, Benazir returned to Pakistan. But shortly after, in 1977, her father was overthrown as prime minister in a military coup by the general Muhammad Zia-ul-Haq. Though the Bhutto family appealed to the international political community for help, two years later, in 1979, Benazir's father was executed.

Benazir Bhutto spent the next several years a prisoner of General Zia-ul-Haq's government, sometimes kept under house arrest, sometimes in jail, and for several months, kept in solitary confinement in a blisteringly hot desert prison cell. In 1984, while living in exile in England, Bhutto became the leader of the Pakistan People's Party (PPP), the first woman in Pakistan to head a major political party. She began advocating for democracy in Pakistan and the ouster of General Zia-ul-Haq.

Zia-ul-Haq resisted and held onto his power, but in 1988, his private plane crashed under mysterious circumstances, killing him. Bhutto returned to Pakistan and quickly won election to the office of prime minister. (Not only was she the first female prime minister of Pakistan, but in 1990, she gave birth to a son, becoming the first modern political head of state to give birth while in office.)

Bhutto served as prime minister for two years, then was defeated in the next election. She stayed involved in politics, though, leading the opposition party, and in 1993, was again elected prime minister. Her politics favored deregulating the economy, building nuclear weapons, and building relationships with other nations. She also advocated women's rights, arguing that a woman who cannot plan her own life is not free, but she failed to repeal the internationally criticized Hudood Ordinance, which established punishments based on Sharia law for extramarital sex, theft, and prohibition. Under the law, for example, rape survivors face a charge of adultery if they cannot provide four, upright male witnesses to the crime. The punishment for adultery is death by stoning or public whipping.

In 1996, amid many scandals, Bhutto was ousted from office, and again fled Pakistan. She remained in the public sphere, speaking, writing, and advocating for the Pakistani people. In 2007, she made a deal to return to her home country and began making arrangements to again run for office. But on December 27, 2007, she was assassinated at a campaign rally. Terrorist group al-Qaeda took responsibility for the killing, but many conspiracy theories abound, some even pointing to her husband, Asif Ali Zardari, a businessman who had been accused of many crimes himself.

Regardless of the circumstances of her death, Benazir Bhutto left behind a complex legacy. She lived a tumultuous life and was integral in shaping modern Pakistan—she even backed the Taliban in the 1990s, hoping they could stabilize Afghanistan—for good and bad. As a woman leader in a region where that is rare, and as a vibrant character with an exciting story, she undoubtedly would have been of much interest to a young, intelligent girl like Malala Yousafzai.

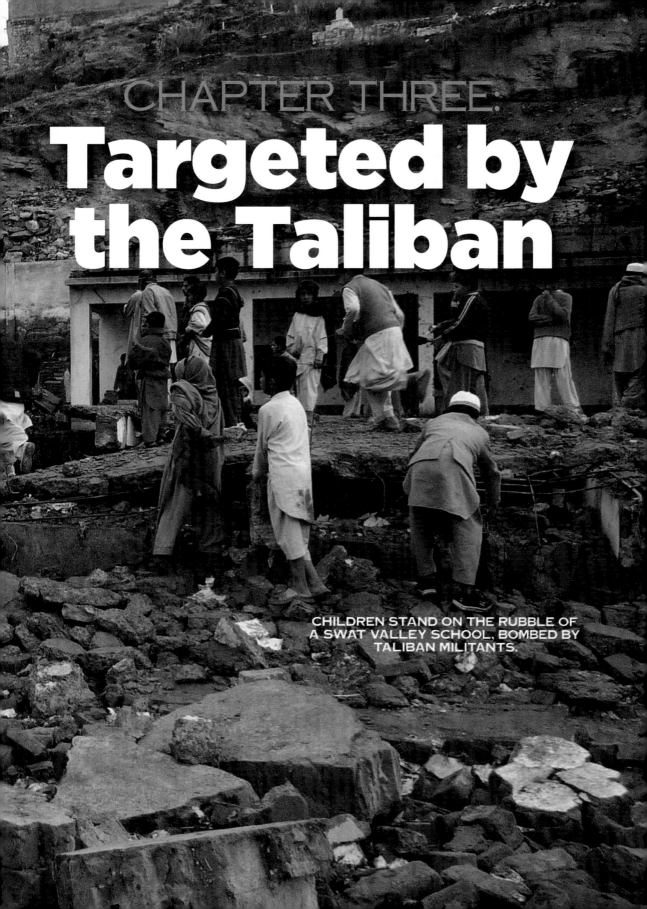

CHAPTER THREE:
Targeted by the Taliban

CHILDREN STAND ON THE RUBBLE OF A SWAT VALLEY SCHOOL, BOMBED BY TALIBAN MILITANTS.

As the war dragged on in Swat Valley, eleven-year-old Malala was prevented from going to school. As such, cynicism crept into her writing. "Five more schools have been destroyed, one of them was near my house," she blogged on January 19, 2009, four days after the Taliban's ban on female education in the region. "I am quite surprised, because these schools were closed so why did they also need to be destroyed?"

Malala complained about the army's inability to oust the Taliban militants. "They are sitting in their bunkers on top of the hills," she wrote of the Pakistani soldiers. "They slaughter goats and eat with pleasure." Malala wrote that she was "quite bored" sitting home all day, and that she could not motivate herself to prepare for exams that she doubted would ever be given. "I do not feel like studying," she wrote.

Boys' schools, which had been closed for a longer-than-normal winter break, opened on February 8. Not so for girls. "I felt hurt on opening my wardrobe and

seeing my uniform, school bag and geometry box," Malala wrote. "Boys' schools are opening tomorrow. But the Taliban have banned girls' education."

Malala's younger brother, after coming home from school on February 8, reported that only six of forty-nine kids had shown up. The hostilities, including artillery shelling that awoke the family in the middle of the night, were damaging her brothers' psyches. Her five-year-old brother dug a "grave" during playtime in his backyard, and one of the boys said he wanted to build an atomic bomb. Malala blogged that one of her brothers "cries while going to school" because "he got scared that he might be kidnapped."

Finally, under national and local pressure, the Taliban permitted girls to go to school beginning February 23. "When I got up I was very happy knowing that I will go to school today," Malala wrote that morning. She noted that twelve of twenty-seven girls in her class had returned. "At school some girls were wearing uniform whereas others were in casual clothes," she wrote. "During assembly girls looked extremely happy and were hugging each other."

GIRLS READ AND SOCIALIZE
OUTSIDE THEIR RECENTLY
RE-OPENED SCHOOL IN MINGORA.

In May, the Pakistani military launched the Second Battle of Swat in an effort to sweep the Taliban militants out of the region. With fighting becoming severe, hundreds of thousands of residents fled Swat Valley, flooding refugee camps. The well-connected Yousafzai family was fortunate enough to stay elsewhere; Malala moved in with relatives in the countryside.

During this time, *New York Times* reporter Adam B. Ellick approached Ziauddin about filming a documentary. In a courageous and dangerous act, Ziauddin and Malala appeared in the documentary, entitled *Class Dismissed: The Death of Female Education.* Malala opens the film by saying, "I want to get my education, and I want to become a doctor. . . ." She pauses, smiles, and buries her face in her hand. Ziauddin smiles and chuckles because he thinks she's being bashful. But then she begins to cry.

While still displaced from Mingora, Ziauddin and Malala attended a meeting at a hotel in Islamabad, the Pakistani capital. Ambassador Richard Holbrooke, the American envoy to Pakistan and Afghanistan, was there, and Malala found a seat next to him. Holbrooke, whom Malala described as a "big gruff man with a red face," asked her how old she was. She told him. "Respected Ambassador," Malala said, "I request you, please help us girls to get an education."

Holbrooke laughed. "You already have lots of problems and we are doing lots for you," he told Malala. "We have pledged billions of dollars in economic aid; we are working with your government on providing electricity, gas . . . but your country faces a lot of problems."

Fortunately, the problems in Swat Valley diminished. The Pakistani army expelled the Taliban from Swat, and by August 2009 most of the region's refugees returned home. When they drove back to Mingora, the Yousafzais were overwhelmed by signs of war. Bullet holes riddled building walls, and Malala's school had been occupied by the army. One military member left a letter in

A MINGORA SCHOOL, DAMAGED BY TALIBAN MILITANTS

Ziauddin's office, one that blamed Swat citizens for allowing the Taliban to rise to power: "We have lost so many of the precious lives of our soldiers and this is due to your negligence."

Malala continued to speak out against the Taliban's violence and oppression, conducting multiple interviews and making a second appearance on *Capital Talk* in August 2009. On December 1, the BBC confirmed rumors that Malala had been the famous blogger. News of her courage spread across the region, and other girls teamed with journalists to write about their experiences.

A PAKISTANI TALIBAN COMMANDER WITH A MACHINE GUN

As Swat fell out of the international spotlight, Malala kept a relatively low profile for two years. She cherished her time in school, where she accumulated gold-colored plastic trophies for her proficiency in English, Urdu, science, and other classes. Within the sanctuary of the Khushal School, she gossiped, laughed, and danced with her schoolgirl friends.

In late 2011, Malala began to be recognized for her activism, first with a nomination for the International Children's Peace Prize by the KidsRights Foundation. The nomination by Archbishop Desmond Tutu read, "Malala dared to stand up for herself and other girls and used national and international media to let the world know girls should also have the right to go to school." Two months later, Pakistan prime minister Yousuf Raza Gilani awarded her the National Peace Award for Youth. At the ceremony, Malala said she hoped to one day start a national party to promote education.

Though the Taliban had lost influence in Swat, they continued to make their presence known. In 2012, Taliban militants crossed into Pakistan from Afghanistan and beheaded seventeen Pakistani soldiers. The Taliban did not just target military men. They also threatened Malala, publishing death threats in newspapers, posting them on her Facebook page, and slipping them under her door. The family ignored them, although she lived in daily fear.

Sirajuddin Ahmad, a spokesperson for the Swat Taliban, which was displaced to Afghanistan, said that Taliban leaders had met in mid-2012 and unanimously agreed to kill Malala. "We had no intentions to kill her but were forced when she would not stop [speaking against us]," Ahmad said.

THE TALIBAN

The Taliban (alternately spelled Taleban) formed in the aftermath of the
Soviet war in Afghanistan (1979-1989). Their name meaning "students" in the
Afghani Pashto language ("Talib" is the singular form), they began strongly
asserting their influence in the early 1990s. At that time, much of Afghanistan
was in chaos following the years of war, with cruel warlords ruling over many
regions and committing atrocities against the people. The Taliban, a loosely
organized movement of religious school students, who had been trained to
fight during the war and were poor and hungry, came together to fight back.

Initially, they were largely welcomed and embraced by the people, as they helped stabilize the region and bring the warlords to justice. But as they gained power and influence, they began forcing their will on the areas they controlled. They favored a highly strict (and according to many more moderate Muslims, wrong) interpretation of the Qur'an and Islamic law, including public execution for murderers and adulterers, and dismemberment for thieves. The Taliban is also openly willing to use violence against anyone they perceive as an enemy; as such, their campaign against Malala was as much motivated by her continual criticism of the Taliban as it was by her activism for education. (In November 2013, the commander behind the attack on the teenage activist was chosen as the leader of the Pakistani Taliban, after a U.S. drone killed the previous chief.)

LEFT: THE REVOLUTIONARY ASSOCIATION OF THE WOMEN OF AFGHANISTAN (RAWA) RALLY AGAINST THE TALIBAN IN PESHAWAR, PAKISTAN.

A TALIBAN MEMBER BEATS A WOMAN IN KABUL, AFGHANISTAN, FOR REMOVING HER BURQA IN PUBLIC.

Malala feared being assassinated. She took a bus home from school each day, and she worried about being attacked while walking from the bus stop to her house. She often mused about how she would address her assassin:

I USED TO THINK THAT THE TALIB WOULD COME AND HE WOULD JUST KILL ME. BUT THEN I SAID, "IF HE COMES, WHAT WOULD YOU DO, MALALA?" THEN I WOULD REPLY TO MYSELF, "MALALA, JUST TAKE A SHOE AND HIT HIM." BUT THEN I SAID, "IF YOU HIT A TALIB WITH YOUR SHOE, THEN THERE WOULD BE NO DIFFERENCE BETWEEN YOU AND THE TALIB. YOU MUST NOT TREAT OTHERS WITH CRUELTY AND THAT MUCH HARSHLY. YOU MUST FIGHT OTHERS BUT THROUGH PEACE AND THROUGH DIALOGUE AND THROUGH EDUCATION." THEN I SAID I WILL TELL HIM HOW IMPORTANT EDUCATION IS AND THAT "I EVEN WANT EDUCATION FOR YOUR CHILDREN AS WELL." AND I WILL TELL HIM, "THAT'S WHAT I WANT TO TELL YOU. NOW DO WHAT YOU WANT."

Malala never had the chance to talk to her attacker. On a hot, sticky afternoon on October 9, 2012, Malala, three teachers, and nearly twenty other students left school in a Toyota TownAce. At one point, the driver was flagged down by a bearded young man with a handkerchief over his face. "Is this the Khushal School bus?" the man asked, even though "Khushal School" was painted on the vehicle. "I need information about some children," the man said.

The students thought the strange man might be a journalist. He walked around to the back of the bus and leaned into a window. "Who is Malala?" he barked. The girls didn't respond, but several shot glances toward Malala. Zeroing in on his target, the would-be assassin pointed a black pistol at Malala's head and fired three shots. She wrote:

THE FIRST WENT THROUGH MY LEFT EYE
SOCKET AND OUT UNDER MY LEFT SHOULDER.
I SLUMPED FORWARD ONTO MONIBA, BLOOD
COMING FROM MY LEFT EAR, SO THE OTHER
TWO BULLETS HIT THE GIRLS NEXT TO ME.
ONE BULLET WENT INTO SHAZIA'S LEFT
HAND. THE THIRD WENT THROUGH HER LEFT
SHOULDER AND INTO THE UPPER RIGHT ARM
OF KAINAT RIAZ.

As Malala waited for help, her blood spilled onto the lap of Moniba, her best friend. At the Combined Military Hospital in Peshawar, where she arrived by helicopter, Malala was rushed to the intensive care unit. No one was sure if she would survive.

WHILE MALALA WAS RUSHED TO THE HOSPITAL, SCHOOLGIRLS THROUGHOUT PAKISTAN PRAYED FOR HER SURVIVAL.

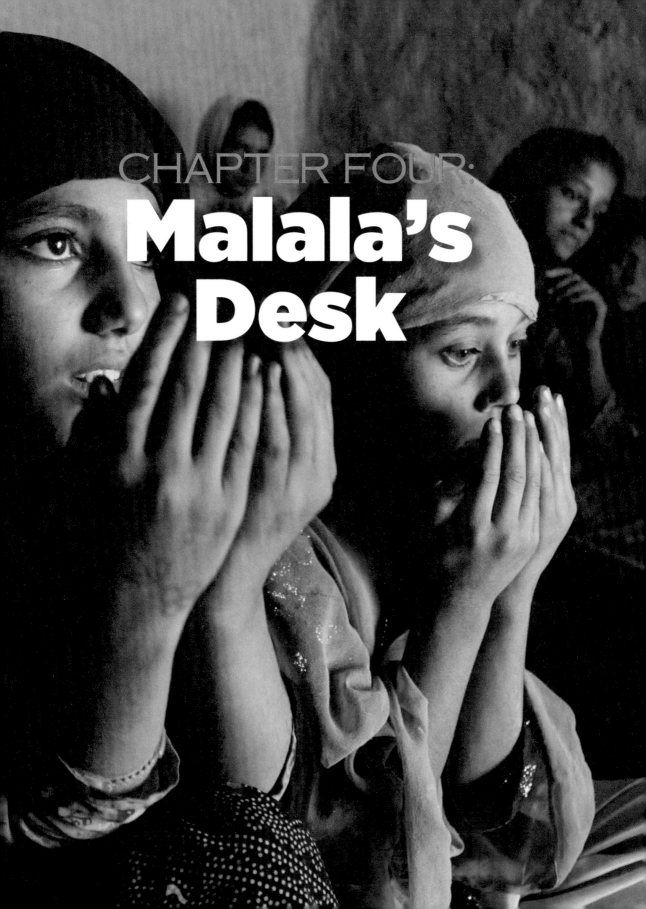

CHAPTER FOUR:
Malala's Desk

As he flew in with Malala to the Combined Military Hospital in Peshawar, Ziauddin Yousafzai called relatives, telling them to prepare for a funeral. Malala was alive but just barely. A bullet had entered her forehead, traveled through her neck, and lodged in her back. "She was initially conscious, but restless and agitated, moving all her limbs," said neurosurgeon Colonel Junaid Khan.

Malala's brain began to swell, and a portion of her skull needed to be removed to save her life. Khan performed the surgery, and although it appeared to be successful, Malala lay in a coma for days. Officials in the United Kingdom offered to treat Malala, and she was flown to a hospital in Birmingham, England, on October 15. There, she awoke from her coma and was pictured holding her teddy bear. Her first words were: "Which country am I in?"

In the days after the shooting, support for Malala poured in from all over the world. U.S. secretary of state Hillary Clinton said that Malala had been "very brave in standing up for the rights of girls." In Pakistan, the government held a "Day of Prayer" for Malala; schoolchildren held hands and prayed for her recovery. Pakistan officials offered a 10 million rupee (more than $100,000) reward for information about the perpetrators, although the shooter would remain at large. Pakistan president Asif Ali Zardari said at a "Stand Up For Malala" event, "We are facing two forces in the country. Malala represents the forces of peace, and we are fighting with the forces of darkness, hatred, and violence."

PAKISTANI SOLDIERS CARRY WOUNDED MALALA OFF OF A MILITARY HELICOPTER.

Most importantly, the attack on the young education activist inspired Pakistanis to action. Many signed petitions that urged the government to pay stipends to parents who educated their daughters. On November 10, dubbed "Malala Day" in Pakistan, the government announced that the families of more than 3 million poor children would indeed receive cash stipends if their children went to school.

Several days later, Pakistan's National Assembly passed the Right to Free and Compulsory Education Bill 2012, which guaranteed free education for all children ages five to sixteen. Under the law, parents who refused to send their children to school could be fined and imprisoned for three months. Those who hired child laborers faced fines and up to six months imprisonment.

Moreover, the government announced it would double the spending on education from 2 percent to 4 percent of national income. "And much of this is due to the influence that Malala and her father and the cause she represents has had on the Pakistani people," said former U.K. prime minister Gordon Brown, the UN special envoy for global education.

Brown teamed with Malala to make people aware of children's issues around the world. He visited her in the hospital and launched a petition, under the slogan "I am Malala," "in support of what Malala fought for." The petition demanded that all of the world's children be in school by 2015.

In a video on his Web site in November 2012, Brown discussed the plight of some 60 million children currently out of schools. Adults were exploiting many of them through child marriage, child labor, and use as soldiers. Millions were confined to the home simply

CHILDREN IN BIRMINGHAM, ENGLAND, SPELL OUT MALALA'S NAME AT A DEMONSTRATION TO SHOW SUPPORT FOR HER AND HER CAUSE.

because they were female. Malala knew the feeling. "I was a girl in a land where rifles are fired in celebration of a son," she wrote in her memoir, "while daughters are hidden away behind a curtain, their role in life simply to prepare food and give birth to children."

In Pakistan, as in many other male-dominated countries, women and girls have endured horrific physical abuse at the hands of men. According to reporting by the Pulitzer Center on Crisis Reporting, Pakistani women and girls suffer from a high rate of rape and acid attacks. Most of this abuse is never reported because the victims are too scared to speak out.

A HARD LIFE

It is hard to be a child in Pakistan and even harder if you're a girl.
Consider this:

- Although child marriage is against the law in Pakistan, 70 percent of girls are married by the age of eighteen and 20 percent by the age of thirteen.

- Pakistan has some of the highest rates of so-called honor killings, known traditionally as *karo kari*, in the world. As many as one thousand women and girls die in "honor" killings annually.

- Pakistan is the third most dangerous place in the world for women—only Afghanistan and the Democratic Republic of the Congo are worse.

- Pakistan has the world's second lowest rate of female employment in the world. Only 22 percent of women age fifteen and older in Pakistan hold jobs, compared with 78 percent of men.

- 90 percent of women in Pakistan face domestic violence, including stove burning and acid attacks, and punishment or retribution by stoning or other physical abuse.

*Figures and statistics courtesy of UNICEF, the Pakistan Bureau of Statistics, Pakistan's Human Rights Commission, the World Economic Forum Gender Parity Report, and TrustLaw, a legal news service run by the Thomson Reuters Foundation.

A PAKISTANI WOMAN, SAIRA, HOLDS A PORTRAIT OF HERSELF FROM BEFORE SHE WAS BURNT WITH ACID BY HER HUSBAND. MARRIED AT FIFTEEN, SAIRA REFUSED TO LIVE WITH THE MAN UNTIL SHE FINISHED SCHOOL, PROMPTING HIM TO ASSAULT HER. SHE HAS UNDERGONE PLASTIC SURGERY NINE TIMES TO TRY AND REPAIR HER SCARS.

Malala has railed against all forms of gender injustice, but her primary focus has been on education. "If nothing changes soon," Brown said in his video, "we are looking at a world where the children of today become the unemployed and unemployable of tomorrow. A world without school is a world without hope. We cannot all be a Malala Yousafzai, but we can all follow her, support her, pray for her."

On December 10, 2012, UNESCO and Pakistan launched the Malala Fund for Girls' Education. Pakistan president Zardari announced that his nation would donate the first $10 million. "Too many girls, in too many countries, are held back simply because they are girls," said UNESCO director-general Irina Bokova. "They are forced to work, they are married off, they are taken away from school. Today, there are 32 million girls out of primary school, and a similar amount out of secondary school. Girls' education is a basic right. It's also a lever for development that benefits the whole of society; girls and boys, men and women."

All of this was happening while Malala was still in the Birmingham hospital. She was not discharged until January 2, 2013, and a month later she underwent another operation to reconstruct her skull and improve her hearing. Malala and her family lived in a temporary home in England, for it was far too dangerous to go back to Pakistan. A Taliban spokesperson told NBC News that they would make an "all out" effort to kill her again.

Though prevented from going back home, Malala was making a monumental impact. The phrase "I Am Malala" appeared on signs and T-shirts all over the world. Thousands signed a petition calling for the heroine to be nominated for the 2012 Nobel Peace Prize. (She would be, and she'd finish runner-up for the award.) In addition, *Time* magazine named Malala the runner-up for its 2012 "Person of the Year," and she won the European Union's Sakharov Prize and its reward of 50,000 euros (about $65,000), a prize given annually to people who stand up for free speech and human rights.

Time noted how Malala had inspired her schoolmates to overcome fear and go to school. "At the very least," *Time* declared, "they will fight for the right of their daughters, and their daughters' daughters, to do the same. Malala's classmates were already brave. She has made them, and girls all over the world, braver still." The two other girls who were shot—Shazia Ramzan, age thirteen, and Kainat Riaz, sixteen—did return to school. "For a long time it seemed fear was in my heart. I couldn't stop it," said Shazia Ramzan. "But now I am not afraid."

While still healing from her wounds, Malala began work on a memoir. Co-written with British journalist Christina Lamb, *I am Malala: The Girl Who Stood Up for Education and was Shot by the Taliban* made its U.S. debut in October 2013, with an initial print run of 125,000.

Not everyone in Pakistan hails Malala as a hero—far from it. Many Pakistanis are resentful or skeptical when they see her meeting with such people as Britain's Queen Elizabeth. Many also feel she has been co-opted by Western "imperialists" who relish in her denunciation of those in her country.

SHAZIA RAMZAN, CAUGHT IN THE CROSSFIRE DURING THE ATTEMPTED MURDER OF MALALA, SHOWS THE SCAR LEFT ON HER HAND BY THE TALIBAN BULLET.

An organization representing 40,000 private schools in Pakistan has banned *I am Malala* from its school libraries. The organization's president, Adeeb Javedan, said: "Everything about Malala is now becoming clear. To me, she is representing the West, not us."

Amad Shaikh, cofounder of MuslimMatters, Inc., believes "that the more significant reason for the negative reaction is an impulse for a people to reject the imposition of 'their' heroes upon 'them.' In other words, a nation likes to make its own heroes and as soon as it is imposed upon it by a foreign party, the first and natural reaction is rejection."

Still others believe that Malala fails to see the real problem in Pakistan: poverty. In many Pakistani families, parents need older children to bring in wages, not report cards. Beenish Ahmed, a reporter in Islamabad, wrote that many low-income parents don't want to send "their kids to public schools, even though they're free. Public school teachers in Pakistan are notorious for skipping class and rowdy kids create havoc in overcrowded classrooms."

Pakistanis also wished Malala would talk about the U.S.-led drone strikes in Pakistan, which have been used in the U.S. "war on terror." On October 11, three days after her memoir was published, Malala did speak out against the drone strikes—to none other than U.S. president Barack Obama.

In October 2013, three months after her UN speech, Malala conducted numerous interviews and met with world leaders, including Britain's Queen Elizabeth. On October 11, three days after her memoir was published, Malala had a one-on-one meeting with U.S. president Barack Obama at the White House. Holding nothing back, Malala expressed her concerns about U.S.-led drone strikes in Pakistan, used in the "war on terror." "Innocent victims are killed in these acts," she said to Obama, "and they lead to resentment among the Pakistani people. If we refocus efforts on education, it will make a big impact."

MALALA MEETS WITH U.S. PRESIDENT
BARACK OBAMA, FIRST LADY MICHELLE
OBAMA, AND THEIR DAUGHTER MALIA IN THE
OVAL OFFICE OF THE WHITE HOUSE.

That same day, Malala and her father sat down with CNN's Christiane Amanpour. In a show that would be titled "The Bravest Girl in the World," Malala expressed her ambitions. "The real goal, the most precious goal that I want to get and for which I am thirsty and for which I want to struggle hard . . . [is to] see every child to go to school," she said. Malala also announced that "I want to become the prime minister of Pakistan . . . because through politics, I can serve my whole country."

MALALA, HER FATHER, ZIAUDDIN YOUSAFZAI, AND CHRISTIANE AMANPOUR POSE FOR PHOTOGRAPHS IN NEW YORK.

Despite her grand aspirations, and what she had endured and accomplished over the previous twelve months, Malala was still a fun-loving Pakistani at heart. "My world has changed," she wrote, "but I have not." Malala added that "my valley remains to me the most beautiful place in the world. . . . I wonder what happened to the mango seed I planted in our garden at Ramadan. I wonder if anyone is watering it so that one day future generations of daughters and sons can enjoy its fruit."

Malala misses talking, dancing, and learning with her friends, and the feeling is mutual. In late 2012, *Time* reported that the ninth-grade classroom at the Khushal School had one empty desk. Malala's best friend, Moniba, inscribed her absent friend's name on the chair's wooden armrest.

"This is Malala's desk," said Moniba. "It will stay empty until she comes back."

PAKISTANI CHILDREN WAVE FROM A BUS LEAVING
SCHOOL IN WAJAH KHIEL, IN SWAT VALLEY, ONE YEAR
AFTER THE TALIBAN TRIED AND FAILED TO SILENCE
MALALA YOUSAFZAI'S DEMAND FOR EDUCATION.

MALALA ATTENDS
HER FIRST DAY AT THE
EDGBASTON HIGH
SCHOOL FOR GIRLS IN
EDGBASTON, BIRMINGHAM,
IN MARCH 2013.

TIMELINE

1997   Born on July 12 in Mingora, in the Swat Valley region of Pakistan.

2008   Speaks out against the Taliban on a radio show.

2009   Begins blogging anonymously for the BBC Urdu Web site about conditions in Swat Valley; Taliban bans and then rescinds education for girls in Swat Valley; the Pakistani military sweeps Taliban militants out of Swat Valley.

2009   Asks Ambassador Richard Holbrooke, the American envoy to Pakistan and Afghanistan, to help Pakistani girls get an education.

2009   Featured, along with father, Ziauddin, in the documentary *Class Dismissed: The Death of Female Education.*

2011   Wins Pakistan's National Peace Award for Youth.

2012   Shot in the head on October 9 by Taliban gunman, but survives the assassination attempt; flown on October 15 to a hospital in Birmingham, England, to recover.

2013   Awarded the International Children's Peace Prize on September 6; *I Am Malala* published; chosen runner-up for the Nobel Peace Prize; meets one-on-one with U.S. president Barack Obama.

SOURCES

CHAPTER 1: THE GIRL WHO COULDN'T BE SILENCED

p. 10,   "The terrorists thought . . ." "Malala Yousafzai's speech at the United Nations," *A World at School*, http://www.aworldatschool.org/pages/the-text-of-malala-yousafzais-speech-at-the-united-nations.

p. 10,   "The extremists are . . ." Ibid.

p. 12,   "In India, innocent . . ." Ibid.

p. 12,   "We call upon . . ." Ibid.

p. 12,   "So let us . . ." Ibid.

p. 13,   "Malala says it . . ." "Shot Pakistan schoolgirl Malala Yousafzai addresses UN," BBC, July 12, 2013, http://www.bbc.co.uk/news/world-asia-23282662.

CHAPTER 2: TROUBLE IN PARADISE

p. 16,   "He says he . . ." Malala Yousafzai. *I Am Malala: The Girl Who Stood Up for Education and Was Shot by the Taliban* (New York: Little, Brown and Company, 2013), Kindle edition, chap. 1.

p. 16,   "We had no . . ." Ibid.

p. 16,   "Our valley is . . ." Ibid.

p. 17,   "She was precocious . . ." Mishal Husain, "Malala: The girl who was shot for going to school," BBC, October 7, 2013, http://www.bbc.co.uk/news/magazine-24379018.

p. 21,   "Islam has a . . ." "The Taliban's War Against Women," *U.S. Department of State*, November 17, 2001, http://www.state.gov/j/drl/rls/6185.htm.

p. 22,   "How dare the . . ." Yousafzai, *I Am Malala*, Kindle edition, chap. 11

p. 22,   "We played marbles . . ." Ibid.

p. 22,   "I was really . . ." "A Conversation With Pakistani Education Advocate Malala," WNYC, October 18, 2013, http://www.wnyc.org/story/a-conversation-with-pakistani-education-advocate-malala-yousafzai/.

p. 23,   "On my way . . ." Sarah Khan, "Swat: Diary of a Pakistani schoolgirl—BBC Urdu.com," *LUBP*, http://lubpak.com/archives/80945.

p. 23,   "Since today was . . ." Ibid.

CHAPTER 3: TARGETED BY THE TALIBAN

p. 28,   "Five more schools . . ." Khan, "Swat: Diary of a Pakistani schoolgirl—BBC Urdu.com."

p. 28,   "They are sitting . . ." Ibid.

p. 28,   "quite bored . . ." Ibid.

p. 28,   "I do not . . ." Ibid.

pp. 28-29,   "I felt hurt . . ." Ibid.

p. 29,   "cries while going . . ." Ibid.

p. 29,   "When I got . . ." Ibid.

p. 30,   "I want to . . ." Adam B. Ellick and Irfan Ashraf, *Class Dismissed: Malala's Story, The New York Times*, http://www.nytimes.com/video/world/asia/100000001835296/class-dismissed.html.

p. 30,   "big gruff man . . ." Yousafzai, *I Am Malala*, Kindle edition, chap. 15.

p. 30,   "Respected Ambassador, I . . ." Ibid.

p. 30,   "You already have . . ." Ibid.

p. 32,   "We have lost . . ." Ibid., chap. 16.

p. 33,   "Malala dared to . . ." Wajahat S. Khan, Mushtaq Yusufzai, and Alexander Smith, "For Malala Yousufzai, a Nobel Prize could cap a remarkable year since Taliban shooting," *NBCNEWS.com*, October 10, 2013, http://worldnews.nbcnews.com/_news/2013/10/10/20898839-for-malala-yousufzai-a-nobel-prize-could-cap-a-remarkable-year-since-taliban-shooting.

p. 33,   "We had no . . ." Jibran Ahmad, "Taliban's 'Radio Mullah' sent hit squad after Pakistani schoolgirl," Reuters, October 12, 2012, http://mobile.reuters.com/article/topNews/idUSBRE89B0IG20121012?i=5.

p. 36,   "I used to . . ." "*The Daily Show*: Extended Interview: Malala Yousafzai," *YouTube*, October 10, 2013, http://www.youtube.com/watch?v=gjGL6YY6oMs.

p. 37,   "Is this the . . ." Yousafzai, *I Am Malala*, Kindle edition, prologue.

p. 37,   "Who is Malala . . ." Ibid.

p. 37,   "The first went . . ." Ibid.

SOURCES CONTINUED

CHAPTER 4: MALALA'S DESK

p. 40,   "She was initially . . ." Husain, "Malala: The girl who was shot for going to school."

p. 40,   "Which country am . . ." Larisa Brown, "'Thanks for all your support,'" *MailOnline.com*, http://www.dailymail.co.uk/news/article-2219509/Malala-Yousafzai-First-picture-Taliban-shooting-victim-hospital-bed-doctors-say-able-stand.html.

p. 40,   "very brave in . . ." Haris Anwar and Augustine Anthony, "Pakistan Girl Campaigner Critical After Shooting by Taliban," *Businessweek*, October 10, 2012, http://www.businessweek.com/news/2012-10-10/pakistan-girl-campaigner-critical-after-shooting-by-taliban.

p. 40,   "We are facing . . ." "At UNESCO, World Leaders Come Together for Girls' Education," UNESCO, http://unesco.usmission.gov/unesco-malala.html.

p. 42,   "And much of . . ." Abdul Hai Kakar, "Gordon Brown: Malala Proves One Person Can Make A Difference," *Radio Free Europe Radio Liberty*, October 8, 2013, http://www.rferl.org/content/gordon-brown-malala/25129996.html.

p. 42,   "in support of . . ." Murtaza Ali Shah, "Malala admitted to UK hospital for critical treatment," *TheNews*, October 16, 2012, http://www.thenews.com.pk/Todays-News-13-18196-Malala-admitted-to-UK-hospital-for-critical-treatment.

p. 43,   "I was a . . ." Yousafzai, *I Am Malala*, Kindle edition, chap. 1.

p. 46,   "If nothing changes . . ." Sarah Kneezle, "Mark Your Calendars: November 10 Is 'Malala Day,'" *Time*, November 8, 2012, http://world.time.com/2012/11/08/mark-your-calendars-november-10-is-malala-day/.

p. 46,   "Too many girls . . ." "UNESCO and Pakistan launch Malala Fund for Girls' Education," UNESCO, http://www.unesco.org/new/en/unesco/resources/unesco-and-pakistan-launch-malala-fund-for-girls-education/.

p. 46,   "all out" . . ." "Taliban: We still want to kill Malala," *NBCNEWS.com*, October 8, 2013, http://worldnews.nbcnews.com/_news/2013/10/08/20868350-taliban-we-still-want-to-kill-malala.

p. 47,   "At the very . . ."Aryn Baker, "Runner-Up: Malala Yousafzai, the Fighter," *Time*, December 19, 2012, http://poy.time.com/2012/12/19/runner-up-malala-yousafzai-the-fighter/print/.

p. 47,   "For a long . . ." Beenish Ahmed, "The Making (and Breaking) of Malala Yousafzai," Pulitzer Center on Crisis Reporting, December 30, 2012, http://pulitzercenter.org/reporting/pakistan-school-education-children-taliban-economic-development-media-malala-yousafzai.

p. 48,   "Everything about Malala . . ." Lucy Sherriff, "Pakistan Private Schools Ban *I Am Malala* Books as It's a 'Tool of the West,'" *Huffington Post* UK, November 11, 2013, http://www.huffingtonpost.co.uk/2013/11/11/pakistan-private-schools-ban-malala-book_n_4253627.html.

p. 48,   "that the more . . ."Amad Shaikh, "Are Pakistanis Jealous of Nobel Peace Prize Nominee Malala Yusafzai?," *muslimmatters.org*, October 12, 2013, http://muslimmatters.org/2013/10/12/pakistanis-jealous-nobel-peace-prize-nominee-malala-yusafzai/.

p. 48,   "kids to public . . .""Pakistani college student creates shantytown school to change society," PRI, September 3, 2013, http://www.pri.org/stories/2013-09-03/pakistani-college-student-creates-shantytown-school-change-society.

p. 48,   "Innocent victims are . . ." "Malala to Obama: Drone strikes 'fueling terrorism,'" CNN, October 12, 2013, http://www.cnn.com/2013/10/12/politics/obamas-meet-malalas/.

p. 50,   "The real goal . . ." Jonathan Allen, "Pakistani teen who survived Taliban shooting speaks of Nobel hopes," Reuters, October 10, 2013, http://www.reuters.com/article/2013/10/11/usa-nobel-malala-idUSL1N0I106E20131011.

p. 50,   "I want to . . ." Ibid.

p. 51,   "My world has . . ." Yousafzai, *I Am Malala*, Kindle edition, epilogue.

p. 51,   "This is Malala's . . ." Baker, "Runner-Up: Malala Yousafzai, the Fighter."

BIBLIOGRAPHY

"A Conversation With Pakistani Education Advocate Malala." *WNYC*, October 18, 2013. http://www.wnyc.org/story/a-conversation-with-pakistani-education-advocate-malala-yousafzai/.

Ahmad, Jibran. "Taliban's 'Radio Mullah' sent hit squad after Pakistani schoolgirl." Reuters, October 12, 2012. http://mobile.reuters.com/article/topNews/idUSBRE89B0IG20121012?i=5.

Ahmed, Beenish. "The Making (and Breaking) of Malala Yousafzai." Pulitzer Center on Crisis Reporting, December 30, 2012. http://pulitzercenter.org/reporting/pakistan-school-education-children-taliban-economic-development-media-malala-yousafzai.

Ali Shah, Murtaza. "Malala admitted to UK hospital for critical treatment." *TheNews*, October 16, 2012. http://www.thenews.com.pk/Todays-News-13-18196-Malala-admitted-to-UK-hospital-for-critical-treatment.

Allen, Jonathan. "Pakistani teen who survived Taliban shooting speaks of Nobel hopes." Reuters, October 10, 2013. http://www.reuters.com/article/2013/10/11/usa-nobel-malala-idUSL1N0I106E20131011.

Anwar, Haris, and Augustine Anthony. "Pakistan Girl Campaigner Critical After Shooting by Taliban." *Businessweek*, October 10, 2012. http://www.businessweek.com/news/2012-10-10/pakistan-girl-campaigner-critical-after-shooting-by-taliban.

"At UNESCO, World Leaders Come Together for Girls' Education." UNESCO. http://unesco.usmission.gov/unesco-malala.html.

Baker, Aryn. "Runner-Up: Malala Yousafzai, the Fighter." *Time*, December 19, 2012. http://poy.time.com/2012/12/19/runner-up-malala-yousafzai-the-fighter/print/.

Brown, Larisa. "'Thanks for all your support.'" *MailOnline.com*. http://www.dailymail.co.uk/news/article-2219509/Malala-Yousafzai-First-picture-Taliban-shooting-victim-hospital-bed-doctors-say-able-stand.html.

Ellick, Adam B., and Irfan Ashraf. *Class Dismissed: Malala's Story*. New York Times, October 9, 2012. http://www.nytimes.com/video/world/asia/100000001835296/class-dismissed.html.

Hai Kakar, Abdul. "Gordon Brown: Malala Proves One Person Can Make A Difference." *Radio Free Europe Radio Liberty*, October 8, 2013. http://www.rferl.org/content/gordon-brown-malala/25129996.html.

Husain, Mishal. "Malala: The girl who was shot for going to school." BBC, October 7, 2013. http://www.bbc.co.uk/news/magazine-24379018.

Khan, Sarah. "Swat: Diary of a Pakistani schoolgirl—BBC Urdu dot com." *LUBP*, January 19, 2009. http://lubpak.com/archives/80945

Khan, Wajahat S., Mushtaq Yusufzai, and Alexander Smith. "For Malala Yousufzai, a Nobel Prize could cap a remarkable year since Taliban shooting." *NBCNEWS.com*, October 10, 2013. http://worldnews.nbcnews.com/_news/2013/10/10/20898839-for-malala-yousufzai-a-nobel-prize-could-cap-a-remarkable-year-since-taliban-shooting.

Kneezle, Sarah. "Mark Your Calendars: November 10 Is 'Malala Day.'" *Time*, November 8, 2012. http://world.time.com/2012/11/08/mark-your-calendars-november-10-is-malala-day/.

"Malala to Obama: Drone strikes 'fueling terrorism.'" CNN, October 12, 2013. http://www.cnn.com/2013/10/12/politics/obamas-meet-malalas/.

"Malala Yousafzai's speech at the United Nations." A World at School. http://www.aworldatschool.org/pages/the-text-of-malala-yousafzais-speech-at-the-united-nations.

"Pakistani college student creates shantytown school to change society." PRI, September 3, 2013. http://www.pri.org/stories/2013-09-03/pakistani-college-student-creates-shantytown-school-change-society.

Shaikh, Amad. "Are Pakistanis Jealous of Nobel Peace Prize Nominee Malala Yusafzai?" *muslimmatters.org*, October 12, 2013. http://muslimmatters.org/2013/10/12/pakistanis-jealous-nobel-peace-prize-nominee-malala-yusafzai/.

"Shot Pakistan schoolgirl Malala Yousafzai addresses UN." BBC, July 12, 2013. http://www.bbc.co.uk/news/world-asia-23282662.

"Taliban: We still want to kill Malala." *NBCNEWS.com*, October 8, 2013. http://worldnews.nbcnews.com/_news/2013/10/08/20868350-taliban-we-still-want-to-kill-malala.

"The Daily Show: Extended Interview: Malala Yousafzai." *YouTube* video, 16:11. October 10, 2013. http://www.youtube.com/watch?v=gjGL6YY6oMs.

"The Taliban's War Against Women." U.S. Department of State, November 17, 2001. http://www.state.gov/j/drl/rls/6185.htm.

"UNESCO and Pakistan launch Malala Fund for Girls' Education." UNESCO. http://www.unesco.org/new/en/unesco/resources/unesco-and-pakistan-launch-malala-fund-for-girls-education/.

Yousafzai, Malala. *I Am Malala: The Girl Who Stood Up for Education and Was Shot by the Taliban.* New York: Little, Brown and Company, 2013.

WEB SITES

http://www.nytimes.com/video/world/asia/100000001835296/class-dismissed.html
This compelling documentary takes viewers to Mingora, Pakistan, in 2009, as Taliban fighters and Pakistani soldiers wage war in the streets. The filmmakers interview Malala and her father extensively in their home. This is a rare peek into Malala's world, before she was shot and evacuated out of the country.

http://www.malalafund.org/
Besides requesting donations for the Malala Fund, this Web site encourages you to "share your story." People from around the world, including many young people, post their comments, which are viewable. A sample comment: "In the 20th century, oil became one of the world's most important resources. Now we must utilize another important resource. However, this one is not measured in gallons."

http://www.malala-yousafzai.com/
This blog site provides a stream of news stories on Malala, as well as photos and videos. It also welcomes young people to "write for Malala." Those who submit blogs about Malala's causes may end up seeing them published on the site.

INDEX

PHOTO CREDITS